ANIMALS
That Make a Difference!

Lions

Ashley Lee

Explore other books at:
WWW.ENGAGEBOOKS.COM

VANCOUVER, B.C.

e WWW.ENGAGEBOOKS.COM

Lions: Pre-1
Animals That Make a Difference!
Lee, Ashley, 1995
Text © 2025 Engage Books
Design © 2025 Engage Books

Edited by: A.R. Roumanis, and Ashley Lee
Design by: Mandy Christiansen

Text set in Arial Regular.

FIRST EDITION / FIRST PRINTING

library and archives canada cataloguing in publication

Title: Lions / Ashley Lee.
Names: Lee, Ashley, author.
Description: Series statement: Animals that make a difference

Identifiers: Canadiana (print) 20230448542 | Canadiana (ebook) 20230448569
ISBN 978-1-77878-690-7 (hardcover)
ISBN 978-1-77878-699-0 (softcover)

Subjects:
LCSH: Lions—Juvenile literature.
LCSH: Human-animal relationships—Juvenile literature.

Classification: LCC QL737.P94 C38 2025 | DDC J599.885—DC23

This project has been made possible in part
by the Government of Canada.

Canada

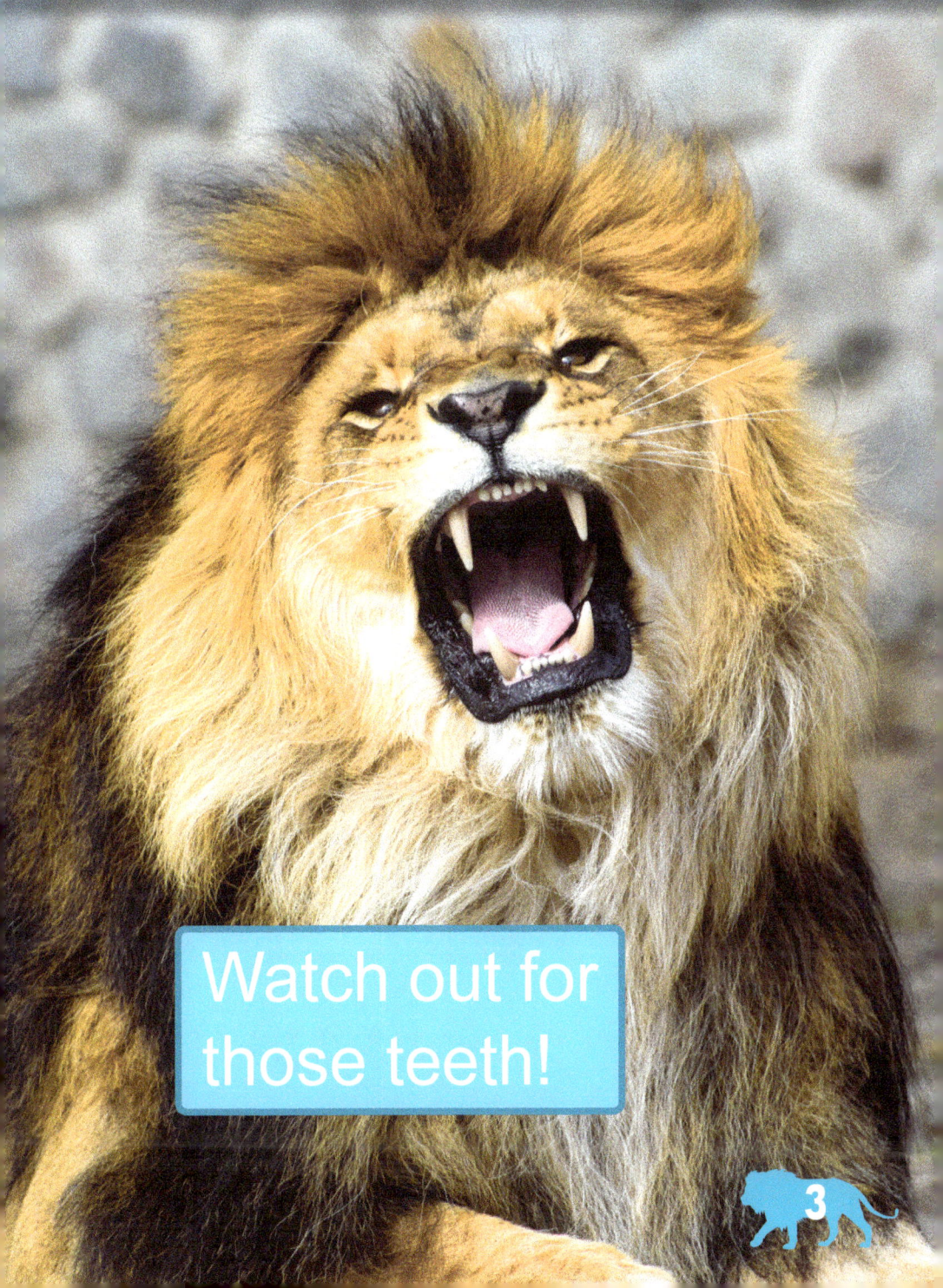

Watch out for those teeth!

Lions are big cats.

They are very strong.

Adult males have manes.

Females do not.

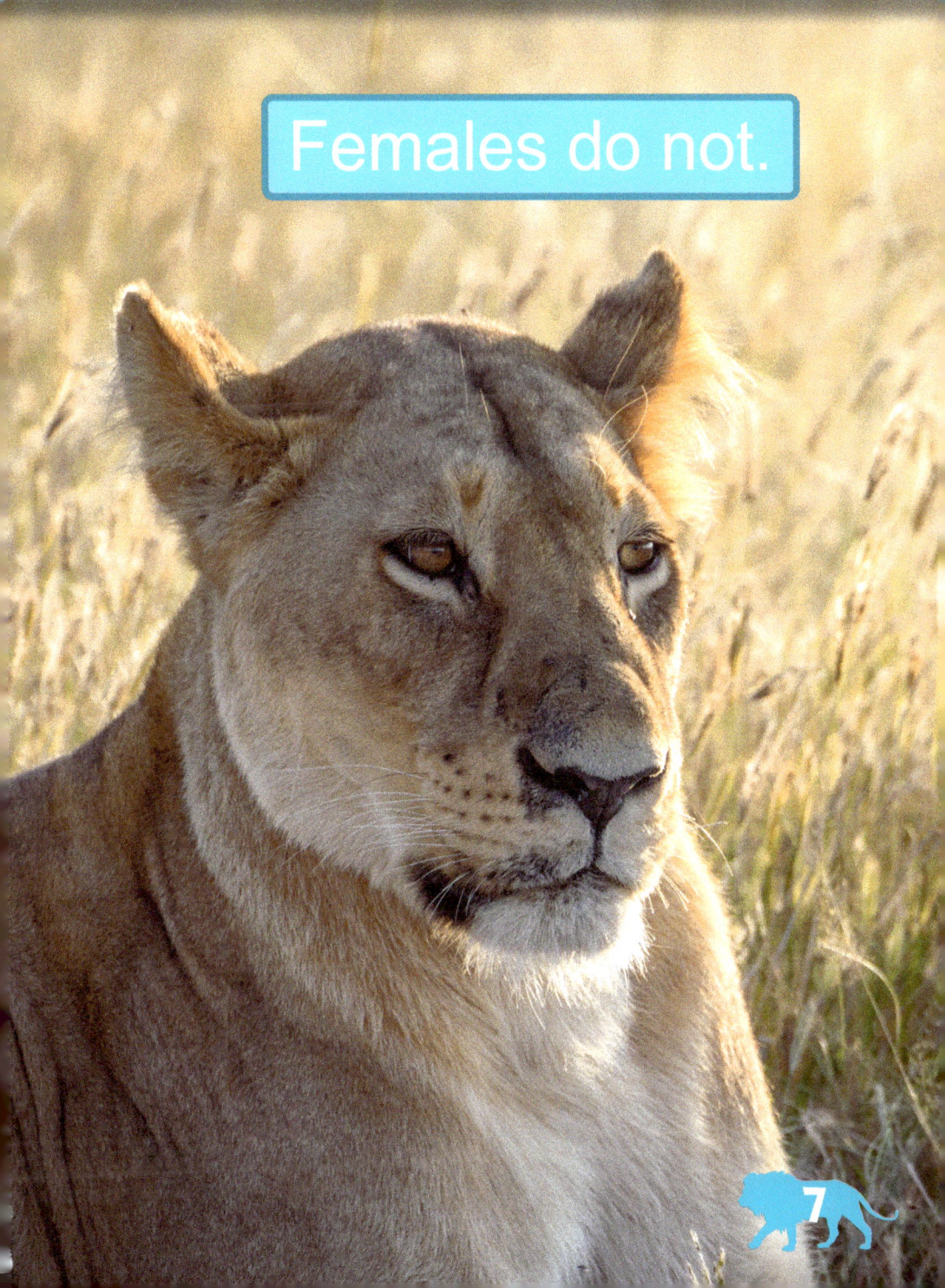

Most lions
live in Africa.

A few live in India.

9

Lions live in grasslands and forests.

They often
live in groups
called prides.

Prides can have up to 30 lions.

Most lions in a
pride are female.

13

Prides can have up to three adult male lions.

Many animals eat plants.

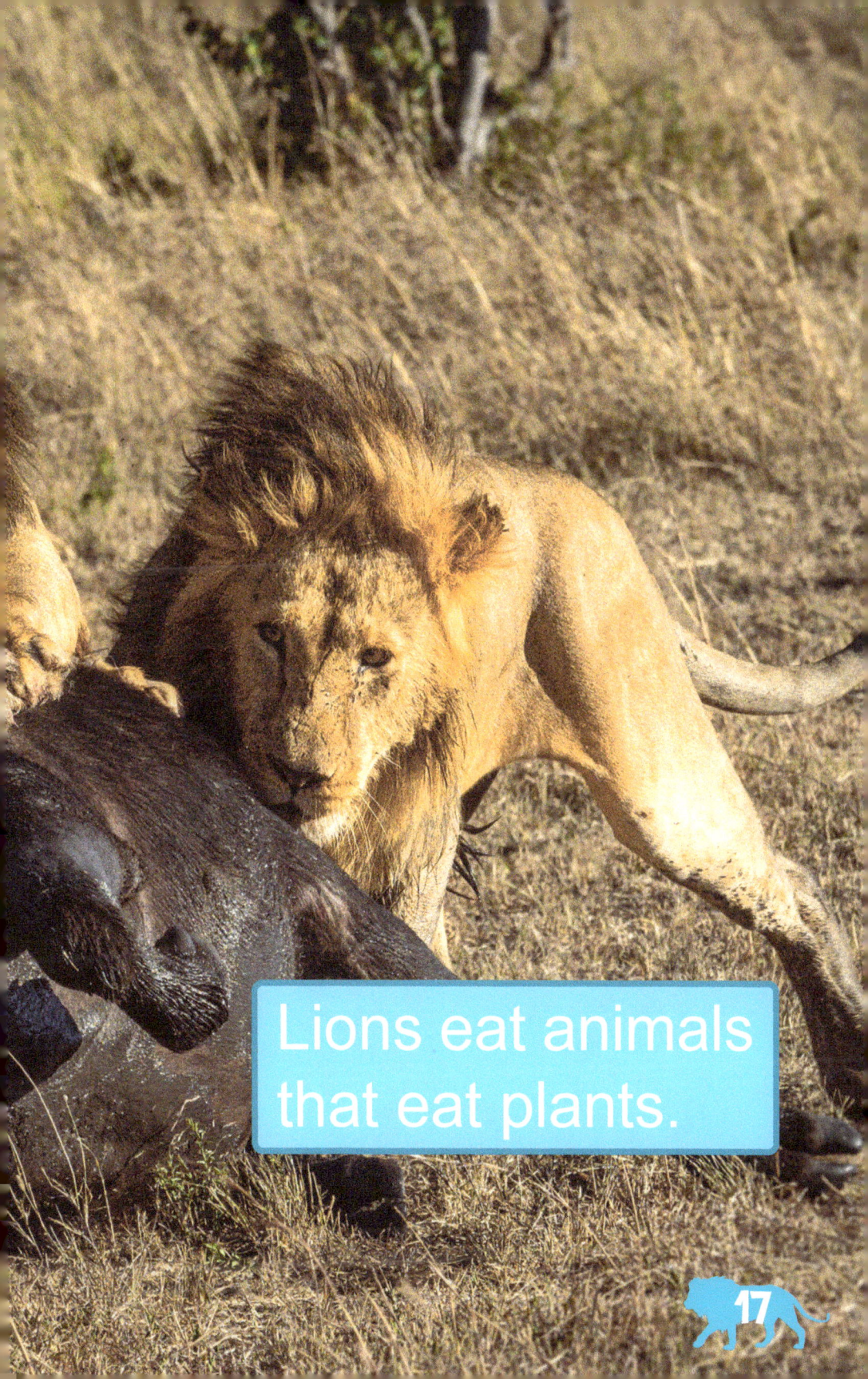

Lions eat animals that eat plants.

This gives plants time to grow back.

This helps make sure there is food for everyone.

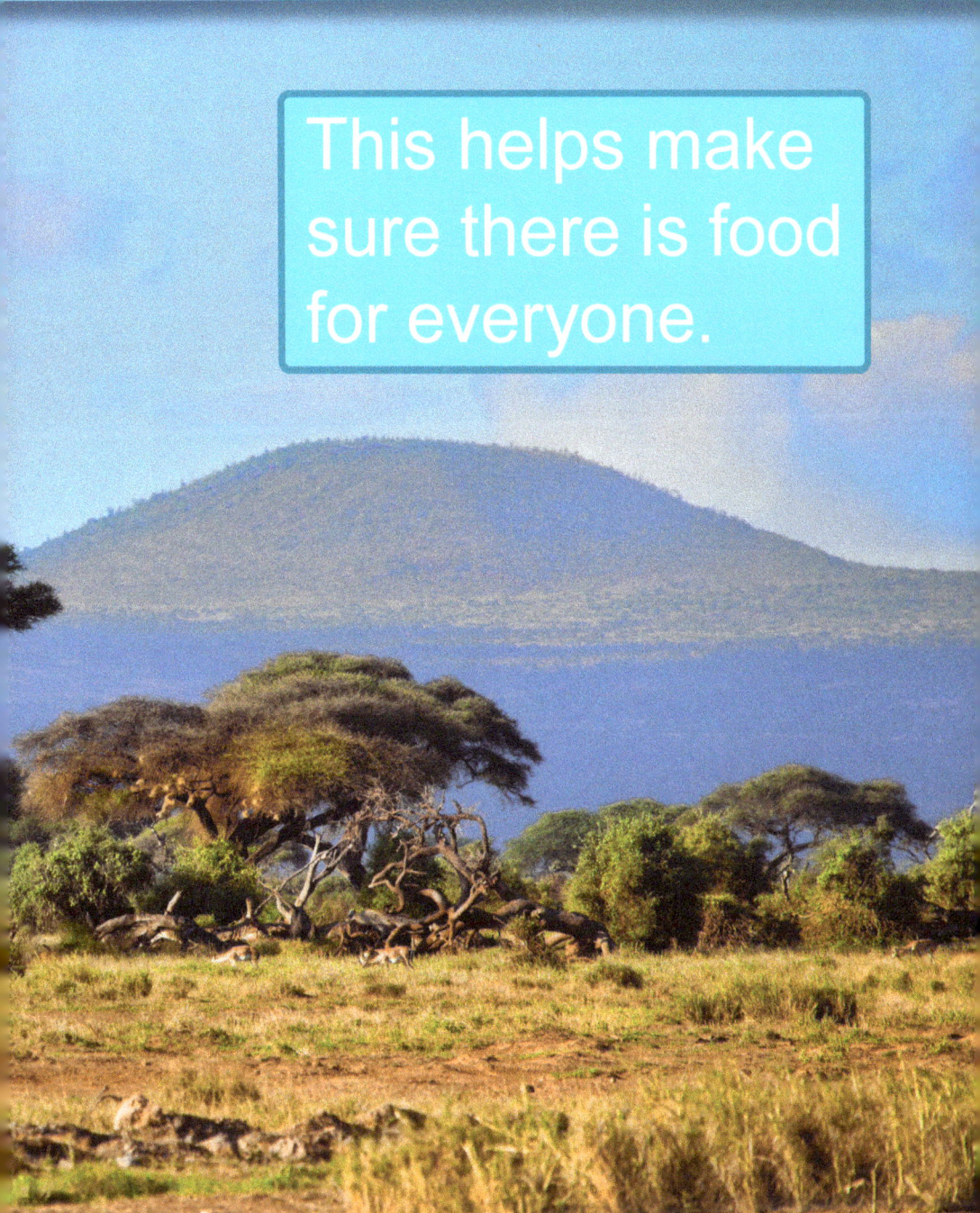

Most lions have babies every two years.

Baby lions are called cubs.

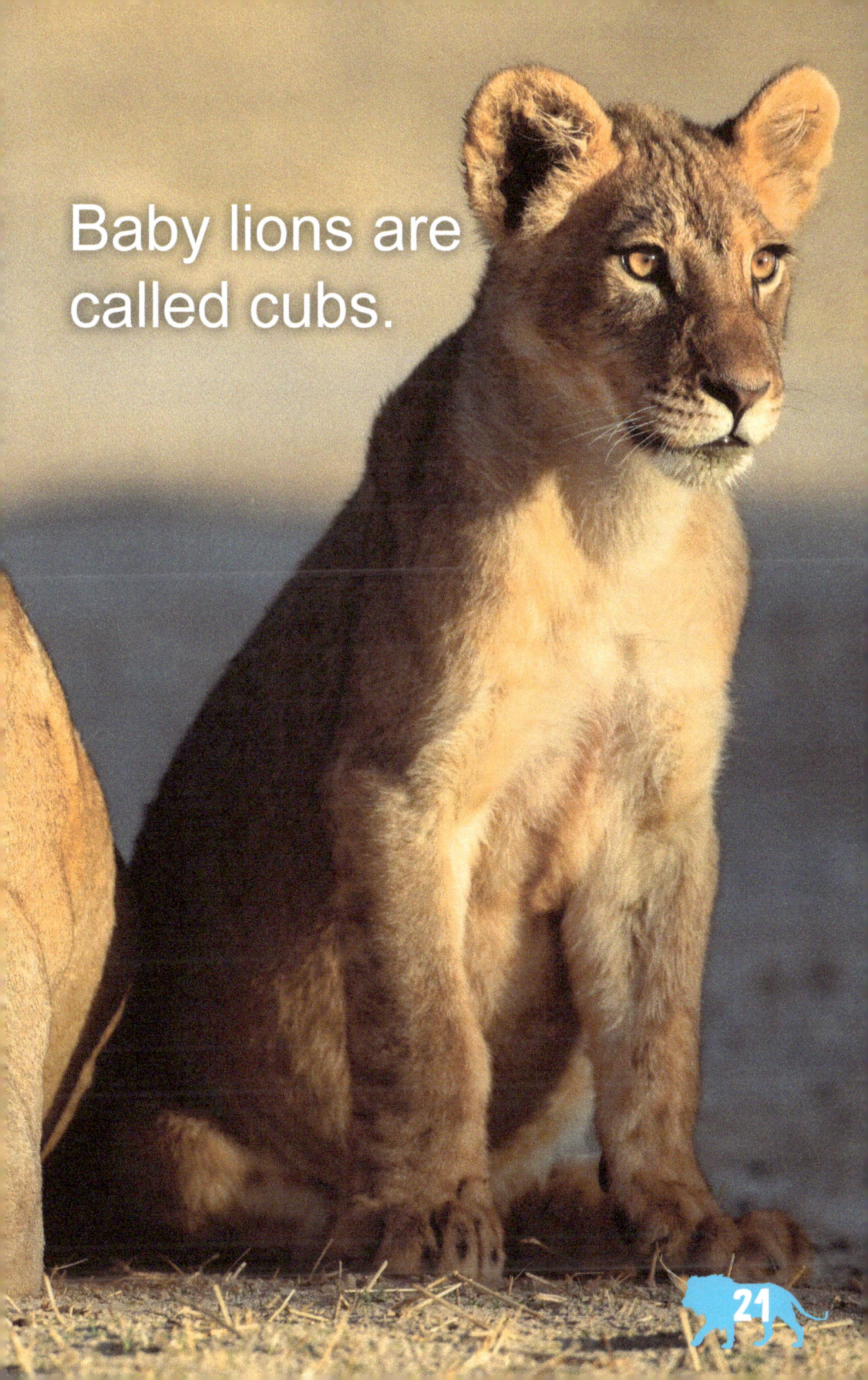

Mother lions can have up to four cubs at a time.

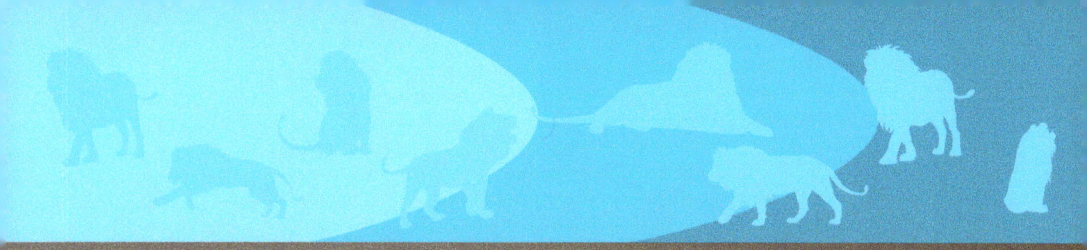

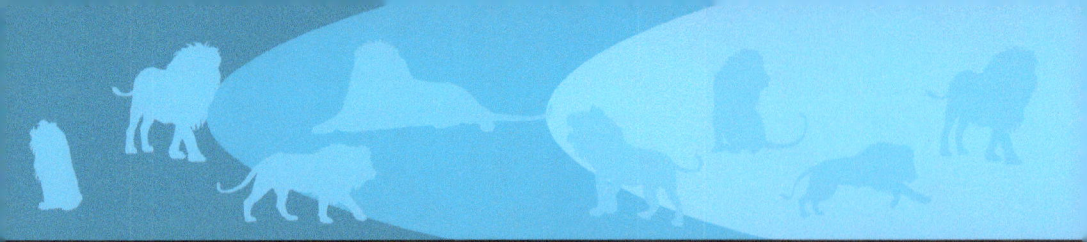

Female lions stay with their family.

Most male lions leave home.

Male lions can live for 12 years.

Female lions can live for 16 years.

The number of
lions is going down.

Many people are working to get their numbers up.

Quiz

Test your knowledge of lions by answering the following questions. The questions are based on what you have read in this book. The answers are listed on the bottom of the next page.

1 Are lions big cats?

2 Do female lions have manes?

3 Are most lions in a pride female?

4 Do lions eat animals that eat plants?

5 Are baby lions called cubs?

6 Is the number of lions going down?

Explore other books in the
Animals That Make a Difference series

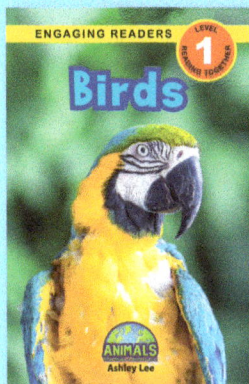

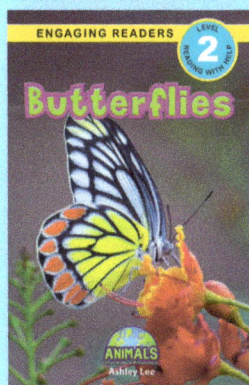

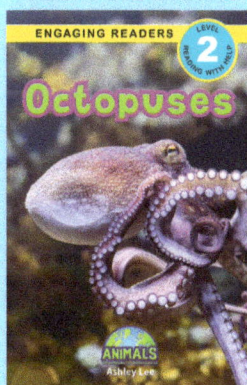

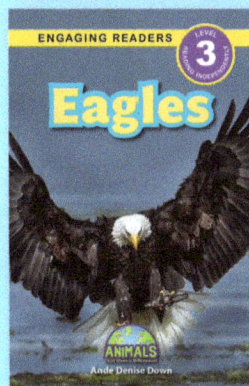

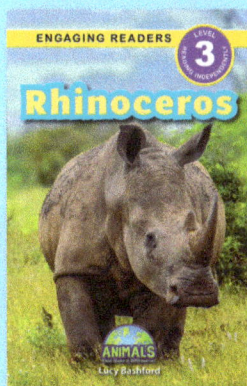

ENGAGING READERS — LEVEL 1 — READING TOGETHER
Birds
ANIMALS
Ashley Lee

ENGAGING READERS — LEVEL 1 — READING TOGETHER
Ladybugs
ANIMALS
Ashley Lee

ENGAGING READERS — LEVEL 1 — READING TOGETHER
Squirrels
ANIMALS
Ashley Lee

ENGAGING READERS — LEVEL 2 — READING WITH HELP
Butterflies
ANIMALS
Ashley Lee

ENGAGING READERS — LEVEL 2 — READING WITH HELP
Frogs
ANIMALS
Ashley Lee

ENGAGING READERS — LEVEL 2 — READING WITH HELP
Octopuses
ANIMALS
Ashley Lee

ENGAGING READERS — LEVEL 3 — READING INDEPENDENTLY
Eagles
ANIMALS
Ande Denise Down

ENGAGING READERS — LEVEL 3 — READING INDEPENDENTLY
Ravens
ANIMALS
AJ Knight

ENGAGING READERS — LEVEL 3 — READING INDEPENDENTLY
Rhinoceros
ANIMALS
Lucy Bashford

Visit www.engagebooks.com to explore more Engaging Readers.